MONSTER MATHS

Test 1	Sequences
Test 2	Multiplying and dividing decimals
Test 3	Equivalent fractions
Test 4	Positive and negative numbers
Test 5	Probability
Test 6	Ratio and proportion
Test 7	Time zones
Test 8	Percentages
Test 9	Angles
Test 10	Ordering mixed numbers
Test 11	Word problems
Test 12	Reflecting shapes
Test 13	Brackets
Test 14	Prime numbers
Test 15	Improper fractions
Test 16	Odd and even numbers
Test 17	Reducing fractions
Test 18	Square numbers
Test 19	Metric units
Test 20	Metric and imperial units
Test 21	Written multiplication
Test 22	Written division
Test 23	Factors
Test 24	Adding and subtracting decimals
Test 25	Perimeter and area
Test 26	Coordinates
Test 27	Decimal fractions
Test 28	Line graphs
Test 29	Frequency tables
Test 30	Mode and range

Christabell
- **HOBBIES** Playing games on her laptop computer
- **SKILL** Technology whizz
- **FAVOURITE COLOURS** Pink and red
- **LIVES** Smile Street with Ezzo, Waldo and Whiffy

Ezzo
- **HOBBIES** Kung fu
- **STRENGTH** Martial Arts expert
- **BEST MOVE** Karate kick
- **FAVOURITE FILMS** Monster action films

Waldo
- **FAVOURITE FOOD** Dog biscuits
- **HOBBIES** Biting squeaky toys
- **STRANGE FACT** Can change shape
- **OWNER** Ezzo

Whiffy
- **FAVOURITE FOOD** Cakes with lots of icing
- **HOBBIES** Playing, dancing
- **STRANGE FACT** Turns to invisible vapour when afraid and makes a terrible smell

P (a.k.a. Princess)
- **HOBBIES** Scheming to take over Monster City
- **STRENGTH** Deadly scream that knocks everybody out
- **LIKES** Sparkly things, parties

Edgar
- **HOBBIES** Making machines to take over Monster City
- **SKILL** Brilliant scientist
- **BEST INVENTION** Gripping bow tie
- **BEST FRIEND** P

Flob
- **HOBBIES** Monster TV
- **BEST FRIEND** P won't let him have friends, because she doesn't want any
- **LIKES** Eating yummy food until his tummy is about to pop

It was a warm summer evening in Monster City. Christabell, Whiffy, Ezzo and his pet Waldo, were chatting happily in the front garden of their house in Smile Street. They didn't notice a helicopter hovering overhead. It was packed with hi-tech spy equipment and tracked their every move. The pilot was Edgar and the passenger was P. Unlike the Smile Street friends, Edgar and P were bad monsters, who lived in a dusty old palace on the edge of town. Their friend Flob, who wasn't quite as bad as them, had stayed at home. The spy equipment crackled into life. "Spy subjects are going to bed", it announced in a mechanical voice.

"Night-night," P cooed ironically. "It's time," Edgar hissed ominously.

Later that night, three shadowy figures crept through the deserted streets of Monster City. When they reached the City Hall, one of them pointed a ray-gun at the building, jamming its alarms. Another figure aimed a harpoon device upwards, shooting a long rope tipped with a grappling hook that lodged on the roof. The figures climbed up and used a laser cutter to make a hole in the Mayor's office window. Before they left, one of them sprayed an unusual and smelly perfume around the room.

Who has broken into the Mayor's office? Take the harpoon device sticker and put it into the police file sheet at the front of the book, as your first clue!

 ## Sequences

If the friendly monsters from Smile Street had been looking carefully, they'd have seen Edgar's helicopter. Looking carefully will help you to spot the missing numbers in number sequences, too. Look at this sequence.

2 4 6 8 10 12

You probably noticed that each number is 2 more than the last one.

How about this one?

3 6 9 12 15 18

 ## Multiplying and dividing decimals

Whoever broke into City Hall had gone to a lot of trouble. Thankfully, multiplying decimals by 10 or 100 is no trouble at all! When you multiply by 10, each digit moves 1 place to the left. When you multiply by 100, each digit moves 2 places to the left. But the decimal point always stays where it is.

H	T	U		Thth	Hth
		3	.	0	3

$\times 100$

| 3 | 0 | 3 | . | 0 |

$3.03 \times 100 = 303$

To divide by 10 or 100, simply move the digits 1 or 2 places to the right.

U		Tth	Hth	Thth
3	.	5	2	

$\div 10$

| 0 | . | 3 | 5 | 2 |

$3.52 \div 10 = 0.352$

Find the pattern in each number series and fill in the gaps to complete it.

1. 0.2 0.4 0.6 0.8 (0.10) (0.12) (0.16)
2. 0.1 0.2 0.3 0.4 (0.5) (0.6) (0.7)
3. 0.5 1 1.5 2 (0.5) (3) (0.5)
4. 1.75 1.5 1.25 1 ( ) ( ) ( )
5. 1 4 8 13 ( ) ( ) ( )
6. 0 3 6 9 (12) (15) (18)
7. 0 2 4 6 (8) (10) (12)
8. 4 8 12 16 (20) (24) (28)

9. 7 14 21 28 (35) (62) (49)
10. 3 7 11 15 (19) (23) (27)
11. 5 10 15 20 (25) (30) (35)
12. 2.2 2.0 1.8 1.6 (1.5) (1.4) (1.3)
13. 12.5 12 11.5 11 (10.5) (10) (9.5)
14. 11.4 11.3 11.2 11.1 (10.) ( ) ( )
15. 3.75 3.5 3.25 3.0 (2.75) (2.5) (2.25)

Write down the answers to these multiplication and division problems. Use the rules opposite to help.

1. $0.3 \times 10 =$
2. $0.02 \times 10 =$
3. $0.125 \times 10 =$
4. $0.6 \div 10 =$
5. $3.3 \div 10 =$
6. $19.89 \div 10 =$
7. $14.01 \div 10 =$
8. $0.070 \times 100 =$
9. $0.034 \times 100 =$
10. $0.942 \times 100 =$
11. $0.002 \times 100 =$
12. $92.1 \div 10 =$
13. $104.8 \div 10 =$
14. $242.3 \div 10 =$
15. $999.1 \div 10 =$

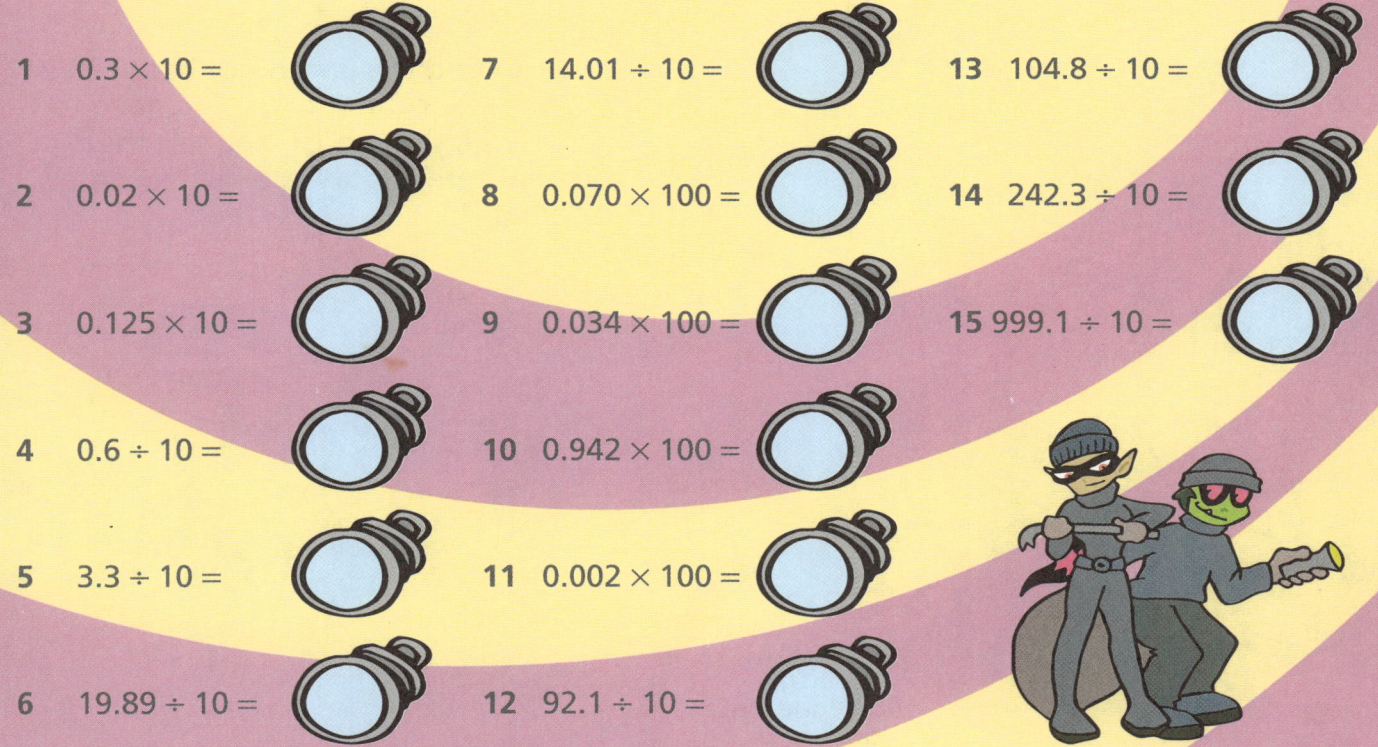

The next morning, the local TV news reported a daring raid on the City Hall. The Mayor's gold chains of office had been snatched.

"The only evidence was a terrible smell," the TV announcer explained. Christabell, Whiffy, Ezzo and Waldo raced to the crime scene to help. The police looked suspiciously at Whiffy, who had an unusual odour.

"Is there a problem, officer?" asked Ezzo.

"There was a Whiffy-type smell at the scene of the crime," the officer informed them. "You'd better watch your step," he said, glowering at the friendly monster.

By the time the Smile Street friends got home, there was worse news.

"Graffiti shame!" the TV reports began. Graffiti had been found all over City Park on benches, walls and even the bandstand. The cameras zoomed in to show some examples. "Christabell was here", said one. "Smile Street girls rule," said another.

"I'd never do that!" gasped Christabell.

"Don't worry. We'll explain that you've been with us all the time," Ezzo reassured her. But as he spoke they heard the sound of police sirens getting closer.

Poor Whiffy! Someone has set him up with some Whiffy smell spray! Add the sticker to the picture.

3 Equivalent fractions

The person who broke into City Hall and blamed it on Whiffy had done something very improper. An improper fraction has a larger top number than bottom number, so it is "top heavy" - for example, $\frac{11}{6}$. You can turn $\frac{11}{6}$ into a mixed number like this:

$$\frac{11}{6}$$

$11 \div 6 = 1$ (whole) with 5 (parts) remaining.

$$\frac{11}{6} = 1\frac{5}{6}$$

4 Positive and negative numbers

The police have sophisticated machinery to measure the smell at the crime scene. It's called a pongometer! But they need to find the difference between readings.

You can find the difference between 2 numbers by counting on. You need to be careful, though. Sometimes the numbers are negative, which means less than 1!

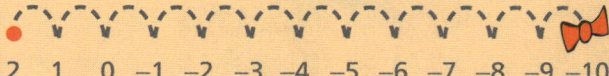

2 1 0 −1 −2 −3 −4 −5 −6 −7 −8 −9 −10

The difference between 2 and −10 is 12.

Look at each pair of numbers. Tick the one that matches the mixed number in bold. You might find the first one quite easy!

1. **1 5/6** — 11/6 ◉   9/6 ◉
2. **11 1/2** — 21/2 ◉   23/2 ◉
3. **2 3/4** — 9/4 ◉   11/4 ◉
4. **1 18/23** — 41/23 ◉ 43/23 ◉
5. **2 14/15** — 42/15 ◉ 44/15 ◉
6. **4 1/8** — 33/8 ◉   28/8 ◉
7. **8 1/2** — 15/2 ◉   17/2 ◉
8. **12 2/3** — 38/3 ◉   38/2 ◉

9. **4 2/7** — 28/7 ◉   30/7 ◉
10. **9 2/7** — 67/7 ◉   65/7 ◉
11. **6 2/5** — 32/5 ◉   36/5 ◉
12. **1 17/35** — 52/35 ◉ 17/35 ◉
13. **9 1/4** — 37/4 ◉   37/5 ◉
14. **11 1/7** — 78/7 ◉   77/7 ◉
15. **14 2/3** — 44/3 ◉   42/3 ◉

Help the Monster City Police write down the difference between each pongometer reading.

	Reading 1	Reading 2	Difference			Reading 1	Reading 2	Difference
1	4	−3		9		−21	−114	
2	12	−12		10		−86	−78	
3	21	−72		11		−53	−123	
4	123	−104		12		−90	−152	
5	262	−201		13		−14	−28	
6	114	−114		14		−319	−391	
7	302	−32		15		−203	−294	
8	−3	−12						

Smile Street was surrounded by police cars.

"We're arresting you on charges of burglary," the police said to Whiffy, quickly handcuffing him before he turned to invisible, smelly vapour, which is what he always did when he was frightened.

"We're also arresting Christabell on graffiti charges," they added, and confiscated her handbag (which contained all manner of gadgets) in case she had any weapons hidden it.

Then the police cars drove away, leaving Ezzo and Waldo in total shock.

Back at the palace, P and Edgar were rejoicing at their success. P was trying on the Mayor's gold chains. Edgar was wiping graffiti paint from his hands.

"There's one more Smile Street trap to lay," Edgar grinned.

"Are the cameras all set up?" asked P.

"Yes and the bait's in position. We're going to catch a big fish tonight!" Edgar laughed maniacally.

5 Probability

It seems likely that Whiffy and Christabell are innocent, but will the police realise that? When we study how likely something is, we say we are working out the probability. Working out probabilities is easy.

For example, a dice has 6 numbers on it – 1, 2, 3, 4, 5 and 6. If Ezzo throws the dice, there are 6 possible outcomes. So the probability of him throwing a 4 is 1 in 6.

6 Ratio and proportion

P and Edgar look pretty close to rounding up the 4 Smile Street monsters. With Christabell and Whiffy both in jail, the ratio of free monsters to monsters in jail is 2:2, because 2 are in jail and 2 are free. But the proportion of monsters in jail is 2 in 4.

ratio = 2:2

proportion = 2 in 4

P would love to be Mayor and rule Monster City! Perhaps her greed will be her undoing? Put the gold chains on the police file sheet.

Help the police by writing down the answers to these probabilities.

1 Whiffy has a box of 8 chocolates. 2 have soft centres and 6 have hard centres. What is the probability of him picking a soft centre? _____

2 What is the probability of him picking a hard centre? _____

3 Christabell throws a dice. What is the probability she throws an even number? _____

4 What is the probability she throws a number divisible by 3? _____

5 Ezzo is waiting for an important letter. Assuming it arrives within a week, what is the probability it will arrive on Wednesday? _____

6 What is the probability it will arrive on a day beginning with the letter T? _____

7 Waldo has 9 dog biscuits. If 3 are stale, what is the probability he'll pick a stale one? _____

8 If he picks a fresh one first, what is the probability he'll pick a stale one next? _____

9 Christabell's laptop picks a number from 1 to 10 at random. What is the probability it will pick 7? _____

10 What is the probability the number it picks will be divisible by 4? _____

11 Ezzo has 3 cupboards in his house, and he knows his skateboard is in one of them. What is the probability it will be in the first cupboard he looks in? _____

12 If it isn't in the first cupboard, what is the probability it will be behind the next door he opens? _____

13 Edgar shuffles a pack of 52 cards. What is the probability he'll pick the 8 of Diamonds? _____

14 What is the probability he'll pick an Ace? _____

15 What is the probability he'll pick one of the Spade cards? _____

Write down the correct ratios and proportions.

monster

1 What is the ratio of vowels to consonants in this word? _____

2 What proportion of the letters are vowels? _____

Mayor

3 What is the ratio of vowels to consonants in this word? _____

4 What proportion of the letters are vowels? _____

jail

5 What is the ratio of vowels to consonants in this word? _____

6 What proportion of the letters are vowels? _____

prison

7 What is the ratio of vowels to consonants in this word? _____

8 What proportion of the letters are consonants? _____

graffiti

9 What is the ratio of vowels to consonants in this word? _____

10 What proportion of the letters are consonants? _____

burglary

11 What is the ratio of vowels to consonants in this word? _____

12 What proportion of the letters are consonants? _____

arrested

13 What is the ratio of vowels to consonants in this word? _____

14 What proportion of the letters are vowels? _____

15 What proportion of the letters are consonants? _____

"We can't leave Christabell and Whiffy in jail," Ezzo muttered angrily to Waldo. In the background, the TV news was blaring, full of exaggerated reports painting Christabell and Whiffy as master criminals.

"Ruthless criminal Christabell may get a fifty-year jail sentence!" insisted one reporter. "Nasty thug Whiffy is almost certain to get a hundred years," another suggested.

"We've got to rescue them," Ezzo declared.

That night, Ezzo and Waldo went to the jailhouse. Ezzo used some gadgets he found in Christabell's room. He neutralised the alarm system with a remote-control purple lipstick. Then he used a laser-fitted hairbrush to cut a hole in the roof above the cells. Waldo, who could change shape, stretched himself into a ladder, so that Christabell and Whiffy could quickly climb onto the roof.

"Is this a good idea?" Christabell asked Ezzo worriedly.

"I'm not leaving you to rot in jail," he exclaimed. As they climbed down, infrared cameras filmed their outlines in the gloom.

P may want to be Queen of Monster City, but Christabell is already the queen of gadgets! Add the alarm-jamming lipstick sticker.

7 Time zones

Fifty years in jail is a long time wherever you are, but time can be deceptive. Monster City is on an island in the middle of an ocean. Far away on the mainland are Grime Town and Grot County. These 3 places are so far apart, they are all in different time zones.

8 Percentages

With Ezzo helping them, Christabell and Whiffy are 100% sure to escape. A percentage means the number of parts per 100. You can work out percentages, too. Just break the number into 100 equal parts to find 1%, then multiply by whatever percentage you need to find.

To find 30% of 200:

$$1\% \text{ of } 200$$
$$200 \div 100 = 2$$
$$30 \times 2 = 60$$
$$30\% \text{ of } 200 = 60$$

When it's 3pm in Monster City, it's 5pm in Grime Town and 7pm in Grot County. Using this information, fill in the missing digital clock times.

1. 02:15 MONSTER CITY / __:__ GROT COUNTY
2. 06:30 MONSTER CITY / __:__ GRIME TOWN
3. 11:45 MONSTER CITY / __:__ GRIME TOWN
4. 14:30 MONSTER CITY / __:__ GROT COUNTY
5. 19:12 MONSTER CITY / __:__ GROT COUNTY
6. 23:11 GRIME TOWN / __:__ GROT COUNTY
7. 20:42 GROT COUNTY / __:__ MONSTER CITY
8. 21:01 GRIME TOWN / __:__ GROT COUNTY
9. 22:36 GRIME TOWN / __:__ MONSTER CITY
10. 19:10 GROT COUNTY / __:__ GRIME TOWN
11. 11:32 GRIME TOWN / __:__ MONSTER CITY
12. 23:53 GROT COUNTY / __:__ MONSTER CITY
13. 20:47 GROT COUNTY / __:__ MONSTER CITY
14. 23:21 GRIME TOWN / __:__ MONSTER CITY
15. 04:31 GROT COUNTY / __:__ GRIME TOWN

Write down the answers to these percentages.

1. 10% of 250 _____
2. 25% of 400 _____
3. 15% of 300 _____
4. 50% of 120 _____
5. 95% of 200 _____
6. 30% of £200 _____
7. 40% of £50 _____
8. 5% of £65 _____
9. 22% of £300 _____
10. 47% of 200 _____
11. 50% of 3 metres _____
12. 10% of 2.5 metres _____
13. 40% of 3 kilograms _____
14. 1% of 3 metres _____
15. 12% of 1 metre _____

"Where do we go now?" Whiffy asked worriedly. "We can't return to Smile Street."

Ezzo handed them each a bag. "I've packed clothes and food to last us, until we can prove your innocence," he explained.

They followed him down a series of alleyways to an old building site. "It's deserted and has access to the tunnels under the city," Ezzo told them, pointing to a drain cover.

The next day, the local newspaper headlines screamed, "Smile Street Gang in daring jailbreak" next to a big photograph of them on the roof.

Whiffy saw the newspaper when he went out later, disguised in an old coat and hat found in a street skip. He also saw newly printed posters entitled "Most wanted criminals", with pictures of himself, Christabell, Waldo and Ezzo. They scared him so much he caused a huge stink, but luckily he turned into invisible smelly vapour and escaped before anyone could grab him.

P is no match for Ezzo and Christabell's teamwork. Put the laser cutter sticker in the right place.

9 Angles

It's important to be able to estimate the angles of things, especially when you're a fugitive, or you'd be constantly getting lost in dark tunnels.

There are 360 degrees in a full circle, 180 degrees in a semi-circle and 90 degrees in quarter of a circle. A short way of writing degree is ° – so instead of 90 degrees, we would write 90°.

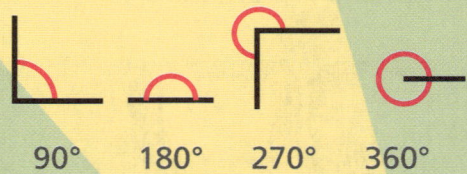

90°   180°   270°   360°

10 Ordering mixed numbers

Ezzo won't want to get muddled with his map directions, as he might fall down a manhole and you shouldn't get muddled with mixed numbers. A mixed number is a whole number plus either decimals or fractions. Decimals like 2.54 and 1.67 are mixed numbers. If you need to put a group of mixed numbers in order, start with the whole numbers first, then order the decimal part, starting with the tenths.

2 is greater than 1, so 2.34 is the biggest number.

.6 is greater than .5, so 1.67 is the next biggest number.

That means 1.59 is the smallest number.

What size are these angles? Write down your estimations.

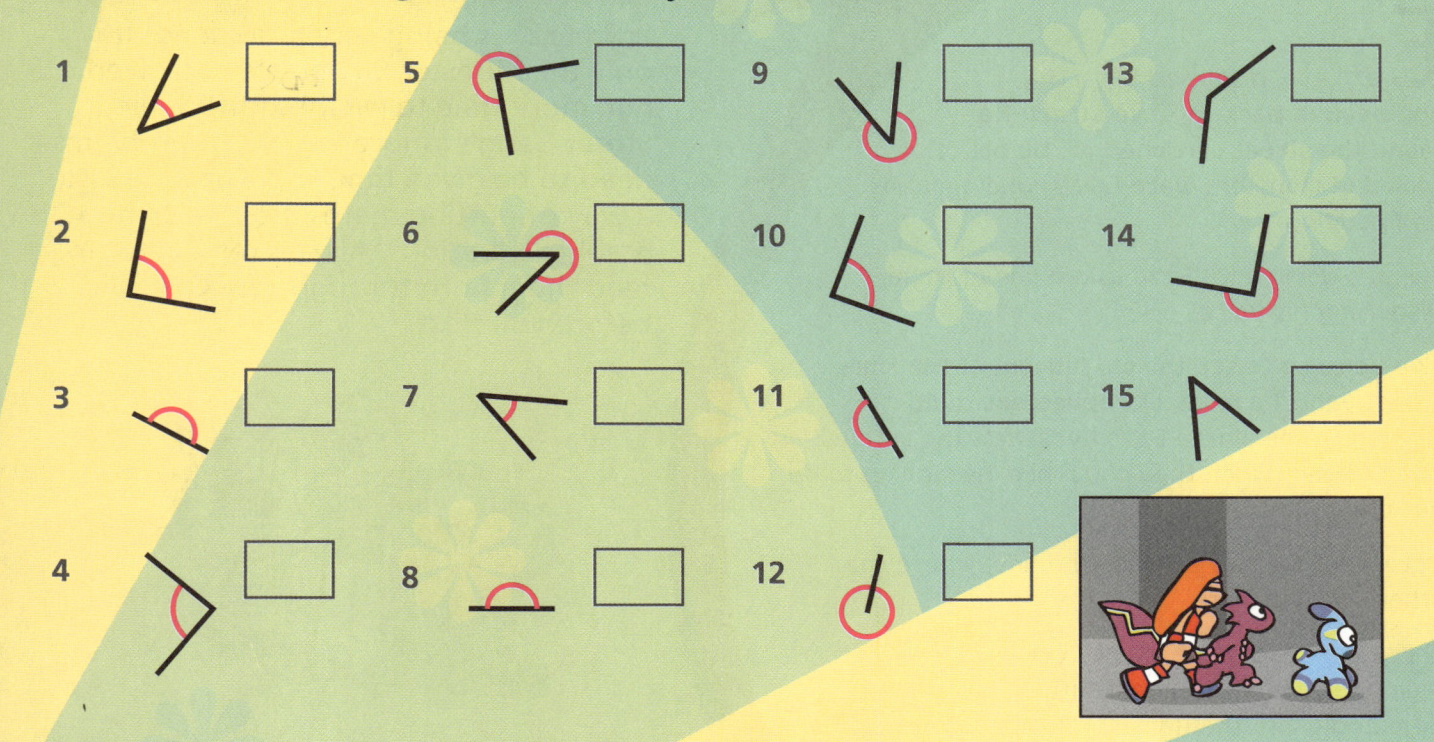

1
2
3
4
5
6
7
8
9
10
11
12
13
14
15

Re-write each group of mixed numbers in order, starting with the smallest.

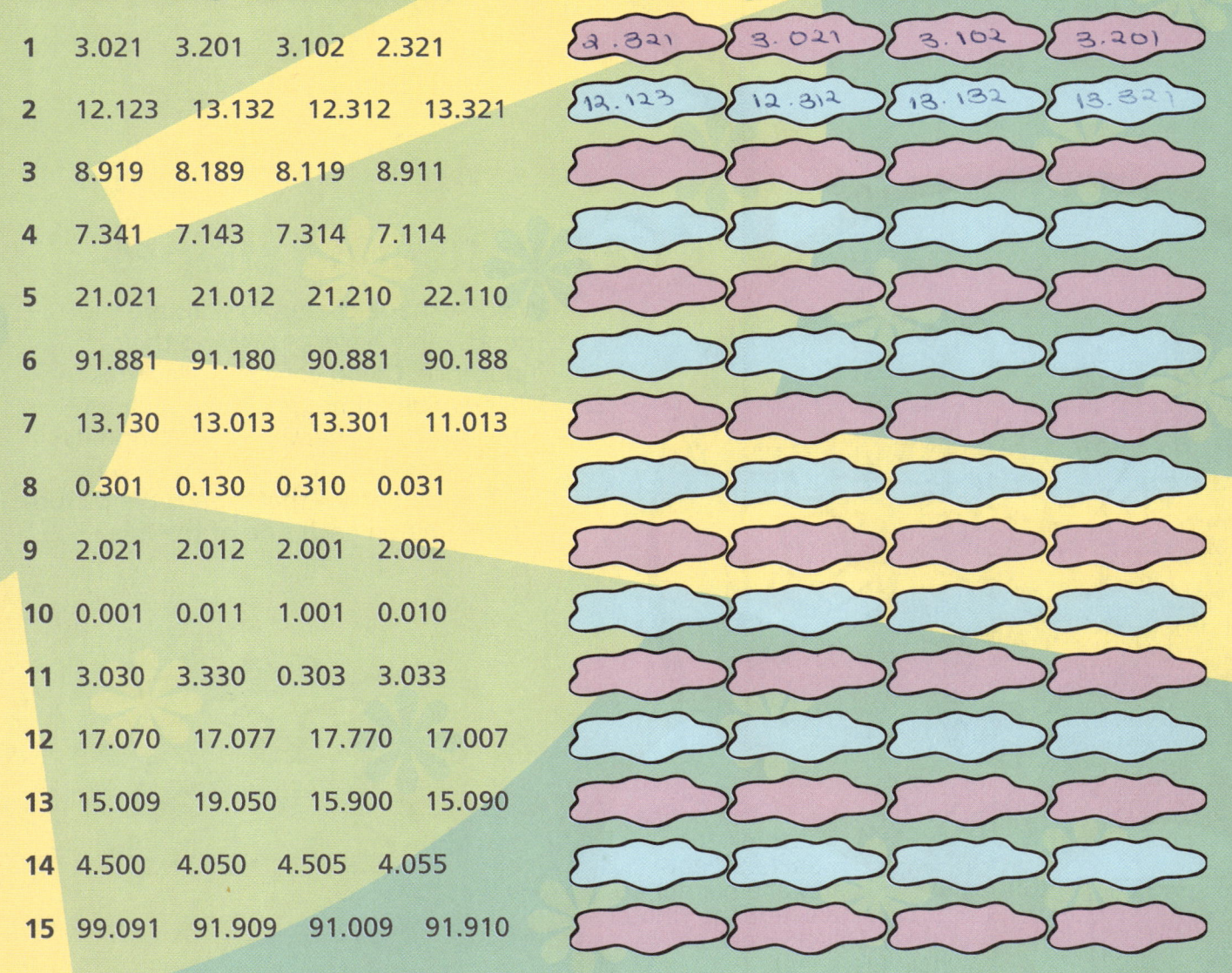

1 3.021   3.201   3.102   2.321   2.321   3.021   3.102   3.201
2 12.123 13.132 12.312 13.321   12.123 12.312 13.132 13.321
3 8.919   8.189   8.119   8.911
4 7.341   7.143   7.314   7.114
5 21.021 21.012 21.210 22.110
6 91.881 91.180 90.881 90.188
7 13.130 13.013 13.301 11.013
8 0.301   0.130   0.310   0.031
9 2.021   2.012   2.001   2.002
10 0.001   0.011   1.001   0.010
11 3.030   3.330   0.303   3.033
12 17.070 17.077 17.770 17.007
13 15.009 19.050 15.900 15.090
14 4.500   4.050   4.505   4.055
15 99.091 91.909 91.009 91.910

Ezzo, too, disguised himself and headed back to Smile Street. He found the street cordoned off by police. A crowd of monsters were taking photographs and pointing.

"What's going on?" Ezzo asked one of them, disguising his voice.

"We've come to see the old hideout of the Smile Street Gang," a monster replied excitedly. "I wanted to see where Ezzo lives. He's the ruthless gang leader. When they catch him, he's going to be locked up forever!"

Ezzo went back to the musty tunnel where the others were hiding.

Christabell had made a small campfire and was trying to cook a sausage. Whiffy was staring dejectedly into the flames. Waldo's big eyes were less shiny than usual and he was so fed up he couldn't even be bothered to change shape to amuse his friends.

11 Word problems

Poor Ezzo is being very misjudged! If only the Monster City police had given him more time to establish the Smile Street Gang's innocence! Word problems need to be given time too. They are just a way of putting maths problems into real-life situations. Always remember to read them right through very carefully before you start.

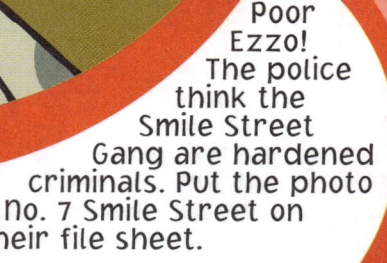

Poor Ezzo! The police think the Smile Street Gang are hardened criminals. Put the photo of No. 7 Smile Street on their file sheet.

12 Reflecting shapes

Waldo's shape-changing skills are the friends' only hope of proving their innocence. Could you be as clever as Waldo? Sometimes, in order to clearly reproduce a shape, we need to find its line of symmetry. The mirror line is the line of symmetry – that means the picture is the same on each side of the line.

Write down the number answers to these word problems.

1. Christabell has 3 packs of sausages and there are 6 sausages in each pack. How many sausages does she have in total? _____

2. If Christabell burns a sausage and Waldo eats one, how many are left? _____

3. Christabell, Waldo, Whiffy and Ezzo share the remaining sausages equally. How many do they each get? _____

4. How many would they have had each if none had been burnt or stolen? _____

5. The Smile Street friends are hidden down a 50-metre tunnel. Exactly halfway down is a doorway. How far down is it in metres? _____

6. Ezzo can sprint the whole length of the tunnel in 7 seconds. How long would it take him to get to the doorway? _____

7. Waldo can run to the doorway in 10 seconds. Who can run faster, Waldo or Ezzo? _____

8. How long would it take Waldo to run 100 metres? _____

9. The Mayor's chains weigh 4 kilograms. If P weighs 80 kilograms, how much would she weigh wearing the chains? _____

10. The chains are made up of 200 links. How much would each link weigh? _____

11. If the chains are a total of 1 metre long, how much would 10 centimetres of chain weigh? _____

12. Ezzo neutralises the jail's alarm for 30 seconds to allow Christabell and Whiffy to escape. If they leave one at a time, how long do they each have to make their escape? _____

13. If Whiffy gets stuck and takes 20 seconds to escape, how long will Christabell have? _____

14. If she has to escape through 50 metres of tunnels and runs at 3 metres per second, will she escape? _____

15. How fast does she need to run to escape in 10 seconds? _____

Draw where these shapes would be after they've been reflected through each mirror line.

The friendly monsters stayed up all night thinking of ways to prove their innocence. By the morning, they had a plan.

"Waldo, it's up to you. You've got to get to the City Hall without being noticed," Ezzo instructed, slipping off the drain cover.

Waldo changed into a bird shape and hopped towards the City Hall. When he arrived, he changed into an envelope shape and posted himself through the letterbox. He was carried up to the Mayor's office with the rest of the mail.

Once inside the empty office, he turned back into his usual shape. He sniffed around for clues, nosing into drawers and cupboards.

At last he found some evidence. An earring lay by the Mayor's waste bin. It still had the faint scent of P on it. She must have dropped it when she stole the gold chains.

It's unlike P to leave a diamond behind! Her greed for power is making her too hasty! Will this evidence clear the Smile Street Gang?

13 Brackets

The Smile Street friends know they need to prioritise their actions if they are going to prove their innocence. Knowing where to start can help you solve problems with brackets, too.

You solve the problem in the bracket first. Then use the answer from inside the bracket to complete the problem.

$$(3 \times 2) + 6 = ?$$
$$3 \times 2 = 6$$
$$6 + 6 = 12$$

14 Prime numbers

Waldo is hunting high and low for anything unusual in the Mayor's office. You can also hunt out unusual numbers.

Prime numbers are strange, as they can only be divided by themselves and 1. Because they can't be divided by 2, they are always odd numbers.

13 is a prime number, as you can't divide 2, 3, 4, 5 or 6 into it without remainders. It can only be exactly divided by itself and 1.

Solve these problems, then write down the answers.

1 (2 × 2) + 6 = 10

2 (3 × 6) − 4 = 14

3 (1 + 8) × 8 = 72

4 (4 + 6) ÷ 2 = 5

5 (9 + 2) × 2 = 22

6 (22 + 2) ÷ 12 = 2

7 33 − (10 × 2) = 13

8 96 − (8 × 8) = 32

9 63 + (3 × 3) = 72

10 49 ÷ (3 + 4) = 7

11 33 ÷ (15 − 4) = 3

12 63 ÷ (11 − 2) = 7

13 27 ÷ (81 ÷ 9) = 3

14 (42 ÷ 2) ÷ 7 = 3

15 48 ÷ (12 ÷ 3) = 12

Look at each sequence and draw a circle around the prime numbers.

1 12   27   ⊙41⊙   99

2 ⊙11⊙   32   21   25

3 35   49   32   ⊙37⊙

4 77   65   17   15

5 23   63   91   75

6 9   1   45   69

7 93   29   27   55

8 15   35   21   83

9 ⊙71⊙   ⊙77⊙   ⊙25⊙   ⊙5⊙

10 33   9   95   97

11 45   33   43   27

12 73   88   45   49

13 87   61   77   35

14 51   53   33   21

15 36   69   31   39

Suddenly, the door opened and the Mayor came in! Waldo turned himself into a briefcase, with the earring safely inside. He sat quietly beside the desk, wondering how to escape.

Eventually the Mayor herself solved Waldo's problem. She picked him up, thinking he was her real briefcase. Then she put him in the back of her car. Waldo quickly changed back to his normal shape and jumped out of the open window when she was looking in the other direction.

Meanwhile, Christabell was at the palace disguised as a flower delivery girl. She knocked on the kitchen door, where Flob was scrubbing graffiti paint out of Edgar's clothes. "Flowers for Flob," she announced.

"Who could have sent me flowers?" Flob asked, startled.

"Why don't you read the label?" Christabell suggested. Flob took the flowers, while she grabbed Edgar's paint-encrusted shoes left on the door mat. By the time Flob had found the blank label, she had gone.

Edgar is so mean, he's made Flob clean his clothes. If he'd cleaned them himself, Christabell couldn't use them as evidence. Add the shoe sticker.

15 Improper fractions

The Mayor solves Waldo's problem for him, but you'll need to master improper fractions for yourself. An improper fraction is the name given to fractions where the denominator (the number at the top) is greater than the numerator (the number at the bottom). Remember, you can turn them into mixed fractions like this:

$$\frac{13}{5}$$
$$13 \div 5 = 2 \text{ with } 3 \text{ remaining}$$
$$\frac{13}{5} = 2\frac{3}{5}$$

16  Odd and even numbers

Poor Flob, who's really quite sweet in his own way, is so busy puzzling over who sent him the flowers that Christabell pinches the evidence from under his nose. You don't have to puzzle over odd and even numbers, like that though. Learning these rules will help you to predict the answers to problems.

1 Whenever you add 2 odd or 2 even numbers, the answer will be even.

2 If you add an odd and an even number, the answer will always be odd.

3 Multiplying 2 even numbers gives an even answer and multiplying 2 odd numbers gives an odd answer, but multiplying an odd and an even number always gives an even number.

Convert these into mixed fractions and write down your answers.

1. $\frac{5}{3}$
2. $\frac{7}{2}$
3. $\frac{9}{4}$
4. $\frac{11}{3}$
5. $\frac{17}{4}$
6. $\frac{21}{5}$
7. $\frac{33}{6}$
8. $\frac{43}{7}$
9. $\frac{29}{5}$
10. $\frac{33}{8}$
11. $\frac{68}{67}$
12. $\frac{41}{7}$
13. $\frac{33}{21}$
14. $\frac{27}{15}$
15. $\frac{53}{17}$

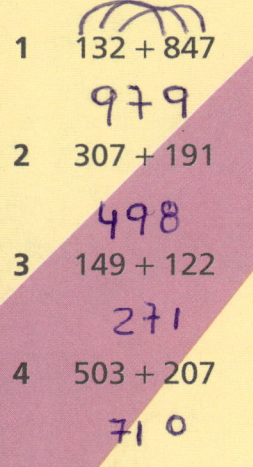
$\frac{20}{10} = 2$

Draw a line from Edgar's shoes to the correct sum.

1. 132 + 847   979
2. 307 + 191   498
3. 149 + 122   271
4. 503 + 207   710
5. 111 + 623   734
6. 128 + 341   469
7. 291 + 114   405
8. 823 + 133   956

ODD: 271, 405, 979, 525, 469, 255, 2301
EVEN: 710, 498, 734, 1426, 594, 266, 516, 956

9. 43 × 12   516
10. 62 × 23   1426
11. 14 × 19   266
12. 17 × 15   255
13. 25 × 21   525
14. 59 × 39   2301
15. 33 × 18   594

As she was leaving by the back gate, Christabell found herself face to face with P.

"Who are you?" P demanded. "Flower delivery for Flob," Christabell muttered.

"I should get flowers, not him!" P cried. She was very good at being dramatic. "And why have you got Edgar's shoes?"

Christabell ran, pressing a lever on a gadget Ezzo had found in her room, which began squirting out superglue. P stepped in the glue and was trapped. She screamed loudly, something else she was very good at. But Christabell was too far down the road to be effected by the ear-splitting noise.

Later, the TV news told of the dramatic break-in at the palace. Reporters interviewed the grief-stricken, overacting P.

"It was awful!" she cried. "Christabell was ruthless! I tried to save my dear friend's precious shoes, but she snatched them from me! I am such a gentle person, so I never fight!" She batted her eyelashes and fluttered her fingers to show how soft and harmless she was. The Mayor immediately sent round flowers and fruit, and P was acclaimed a brave heroine.

Flob is so confused that he's forgotten to clean Edgar's trousers. Pop them on the police file along with the shoes.

17 Reducing fractions

Grabbing Edgar's shoes was easy for Christabell. You can make your life easier, too, if you can reduce fractions to their simplest form. It makes it easier to see what they're really worth and compare them with other fractions. $\frac{4}{12}$ can be made simpler by dividing both the top and the bottom number by 4.

$$4 \div 4 = 1$$
$$12 \div 4 = 3$$
$$\frac{4}{12} = \frac{1}{3}$$

If you can find a number that will divide exactly into the top and the bottom number of a fraction, you can make the fraction simpler.

18 Square numbers

P isn't known for her honesty, but this lie is a real whopper! The Smile Street friends' problems are getting bigger and bigger. You can make numbers bigger instantly by multiplying them by themselves.

$$4 \times 4 = 16$$

16 is the square of 4 (where a number is multiplied by itself) and 4 is the square root of 16.

Write down what these fractions are when reduced to their simplest form. Remember, look for a number that divides exactly into the bottom and the top number.

1 $\frac{2}{4}$    5 $\frac{2}{10}$    9 $\frac{12}{18}$    13 $\frac{6}{14}$

2 $\frac{3}{9}$    6 $\frac{6}{8}$    10 $\frac{10}{15}$    14 $\frac{8}{16}$

3 $\frac{5}{10}$    7 $\frac{6}{9}$  11 $\frac{6}{12}$  15 $\frac{12}{20}$

4 $\frac{4}{8}$  8 $\frac{3}{15}$  12 $\frac{9}{12}$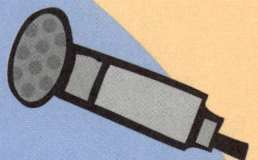

Circle the square number in each line-up. Then write down its square root.

1 114 111 100 102 _____   10 121 74   69   46   _____

2 36   32   33   34   _____   11 91   64   61   59   _____

3 14   4   41   44   _____   12 12   144 31   126 _____

4 6   9   19   11   _____   13 250 2500 2005 2000 _____

5 75   18   25   43   _____   14 71   400 401 393 _____

6 41   49   56   99   _____   15 863 900 701 893 _____

7 81   143 110 72   _____

8 71   123 7   16   _____

9 2   1   17   23   _____

"We have two pieces of evidence to prove P's guilt, but we need more," Ezzo fretted when the friends regrouped in their tunnel hideout.

"A lot more," Whiffy sighed, showing them some newspaper cuttings he'd gathered. Ridiculous crimes were being blamed on the Smile Street friends, from stealing a baby's dummy to stealing the good weather. A reward had been offered for their capture.

"This is getting out of hand," Ezzo crumpled the papers angrily.

"They didn't waste any time," Christabell sighed as she peeped out from under the drain cover. A group of monsters had arrived at the building site and were searching through the rubble. They had "Smile Street Bounty Hunters" written on their T-shirts.

"This is getting too dangerous!" Ezzo whispered. "We need some outside help." They cowered beneath the drain cover, waiting for the hunters to go.

P is jealous of the goodies getting their picture in the papers, so she makes Edgar take some pictures of her in the stolen gold chains. Silly P! Add the sticker.

19 Metric units

It looks like the friends will have to stay in hiding. Let's hope they have enough provisions to last them and that they are hidden deep enough underground. Christabell will need to check the depths of the tunnels by converting the metric units.

Remember, there are …

- 10 millimetres in a centimetre
- 100 centimetres in a metre
- 1000 metres in a kilometre
- 1000 grams in a kilogram
- 1000 millilitres in a litre

Also remember that we can shorten these words:

- millimetre = mm
- centimetre = cm
- metre = m
- kilometre = km
- gram = g
- kilogram = kg
- millilitre = ml
- litre = l

20 Metric and imperial units

Getting the right evidence sometimes means converting measurements. The first chart shows rough equivalents between imperial and metric weights and measurements.

Imperial	Metric
1 oz	25 g
1 lb	450 g
1 pint	550 ml
1 inch	2.5 cm

oz is short for ounce

lb is short for pound

Look at the bold measurements, then circle the one that matches it.

1	**3m**	30cm	300mm	300cm
2	**25cm**	25mm	2.5m	250mm
3	**1.5m**	15cm	150cm	1500cm
4	**3km**	300m	3000m	3000cm
5	**0.5km**	50m	500cm	500m
6	**1m**	1000mm	100m	10cm
7	**250cm**	25m	2.5m	250mm
8	**500g**	5kg	0.5kg	50kg
9	**1500g**	15kg	1.5kg	150kg
10	**3kg**	300g	3000g	30g
11	**6.2kg**	6200g	620g	62g
12	**2l**	200ml	20ml	2000ml
13	**3.5l**	350ml	3500ml	35ml
14	**500ml**	0.5l	5l	50l
15	**750ml**	75l	7.5l	0.75l

Some of the measurements from this chart have faded. Fill them back in again.

	Imperial	Metric
1	_____	900g
2	1 pint	_____
3	_____	100g
4	2 inches	_____
5	_____	550ml
6	3lbs	_____
7	_____	1100ml
8	6oz	_____

	Imperial	Metric
9	_____	7.5cm
10	½ lb	_____
11	_____	250g
12	1.5 pints	_____
13	_____	2.2l
14	3 oz	_____
15	_____	10cm

This time, Whiffy went to the palace. As expected, he turned invisible with fright as he got near. Flob was out in the garden and although he didn't see Whiffy, he could certainly smell him.

"Yaargh!" Flob choked as Whiffy dropped a note written on pink paper into his hands. When Flob recovered, he read the message and the words made him blush deeply. "I can't let it happen. It's not right," he muttered to himself and walked off purposefully.

The next day, another letter arrived at the palace addressed to P and Edgar. "We want a showdown. Come to the old building site if you think you're tough enough." It was signed, "The Smile Street Gang".

"How silly. Of course we're tough enough! Especially as we'll make sure the police are there, too! They'll capture those idiots and that'll be that," Edgar grinned.

"What should I wear to a showdown?" P mused.

"Something glamorous. We'll be inviting TV crews," Edgar added.

"I shall be in the papers again!" said P, as she clapped her hands with delight.

P and Edgar are getting a little too big for their boots! Put their letter into the picture.

Written multiplication

Wonder what's on the paper Whiffy gave Flob? Perhaps Whiffy's been practising his multiplication again! He knows there are 2 written methods you can use for multiplying large numbers.

Written method 1:
18×23

$18 \times 20 = 360 +$
$18 \times 3 = 54$
$ \overline{414}$

Written method 2:
18×23

$ \times 10 \times 8$

$20 \rightarrow 200 \rightarrow 160 360 +$
$3 \rightarrow 30 \rightarrow 24 54$
$ \overline{414}$

Written division

P wants to make sure her defeat of the Smile Street Gang goes down on record. She'd be better off concentrating on putting her division down on paper, like this:

$498 \div 42$

$ \underline{ 11 \text{ r } 36}$
$42 \div 498$
$- 420 (10 \times 42)$
$ 78$
$- 42 (1 \times 42)$
$ \text{r } 36$

r is a short way of writing 'remaining' or 'remainder'.

Use one of Whiffy's methods to work out these problems. (You may need some extra paper for this.) Then write down the answers here.

1 31 × 14 = 434
2 19 × 32 =
3 44 × 66 =
4 57 × 31 =
5 91 × 21 =
6 65 × 23 =

7 72 × 18 =
8 51 × 34 =
9 49 × 40 =
10 27 × 61 =
11 120 × 29 =
12 150 × 41 =

13 125 × 59 =
14 176 × 23 =
15 113 × 35 =

Write down the answers to these division problems. You'll need to concentrate hard, and you may need some spare paper for working out!

1 742 ÷ 32 =
2 571 ÷ 20 =
3 943 ÷ 15 =
4 622 ÷ 39 =
5 381 ÷ 27 =
6 642 ÷ 14 =

7 613 ÷ 43 =
8 729 ÷ 31 =
9 441 ÷ 12 =

10 809 ÷ 32 =
11 561 ÷ 12 =
12 714 ÷ 22 =
13 937 ÷ 38 =
14 414 ÷ 32 =
15 496 ÷ 19 =

P and Edgar went to the deserted building site at nightfall.

"The police and press will be here soon," Edgar muttered nervously.

Suddenly, the Smile Street friends stepped out from the shadows, looking as tough as they could.

"We meet again," hissed Edgar.

"We have evidence against you for the theft of the Mayor's gold chains, P. We have your earring, which you left in the Mayor's office," Christabell announced.

"Hit them with your piercing scream, P," Edgar muttered.

But P couldn't scream, because she had begun to giggle. "Me? In jail? Ha-ha! Of course I stole the chains, but nobody will believe you!" she guffawed.

"We also have Edgar's shoes, splattered with graffiti paint," Ezzo said loudly.

"So what? I know I did it, but shoes don't prove anything," Edgar grinned. Behind him, three of his large robot fighters appeared.

Ezzo leapt through the air and smashed one down with a karate kick. The other two advanced menacingly.

Edgar shouldn't be quite so confident, as his paint splattered shirt has been recovered. Pop it on the file sheet.

23) Factors

Teamwork by the Smile Street friends has meant they have collected enough evidence to prove their innocence, and P and Edgar's guilt. You'll often find numbers working together too, to build bigger numbers. Many numbers are made up of factors. Factors are other numbers that can be divided exactly into them.

18 has several factors:

18 9 6 3 2 1

24) Adding and subtracting decimals

P may have made a huge mistake. You can stop yourself from making a mistake when you're adding or subtracting decimals by keeping an eye on place value. Line up the decimal points and you can't go wrong.

Write down all the factors for each of these numbers.

1 24
2 36
3 50
4 17
5 14
6 84
7 64
8 48

9 56
10 100
11 29
12 55
13 32
14 33
15 96

Re-write these sums so that the numbers are lined up underneath each other in the correct place. Then work out the answers.

Correctly lined up   Answer

1 3.31
   4.01 +

2 7.24
   1.85 +

3 9.01
   0.32 +

4 5.23
   3.71 +

5 6.72
   9.49 +

6 1.89
   3.30 +

7 2.71
   1.48 +

8 10.32
   2.09 +

Correctly lined up   Answer

9 6.74
   4.51 −

10 8.82
    7.11 −

11 12.09
    3.03 −

12 7.31
    3.49 −

13 3.84
    1.99 −

14 10.01
    3.32 −

15 13.42
    4.84 −

Suddenly, everyone was bathed in TV camera floodlights. Helicopters buzzed overhead.

"This is the police!" a voice announced through a megaphone.

"Oh good," P smiled. "Hello!" she waved at the TV cameras.

"We're arresting you, P and Edgar for crimes around Monster City," the megaphone voice shouted. "We had a secret tip-off about you. You've admitted your guilt, live on TV."

"Never!" P cried.

Then she screamed. All those around were momentarily stunned and several TV cameras were broken. When everyone recovered, P and Edgar were gone. The helicopters flew over the town and found them in one of their light beams. Edgar and P were moving towards the palace, where Flob was waiting to speed them away in a fast car.

Ezzo dashed after them, his athletic frame easily keeping up with the helicopters.

"Wow! Look at him go!" the press cried and began taking photos, this time for their sports pages.

The police take photographs of Edgar and P as they run away. Put this valuable piece of evidence onto the right place on the sheet.

25 Perimeter and area

The building site where the showdown takes place is 100m long and 30m wide.

Its perimeter (all the way round the edge) is $100 + 30 + 100 + 30 = 260$m.

Its area (the amount of space it takes up) is $100 \times 30 = 3000$m^2.

m^2 is another way of writing square metres.

26 Coordinates

Ezzo needs to make sure he has a copy of this map if he has any chance of catching Flob.

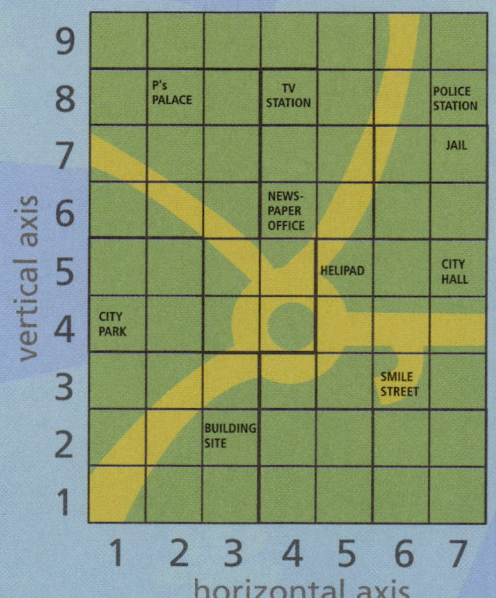

Coordinates help you to pinpoint exactly where a place is on a map. You count letters or numbers on a grid and they tell you the position of particular things or places.

Write down the size of these perimeters and areas.

1 Perimeter = ▢ cm
2 Area = ▢ cm²
   (3cm × 1cm rectangle)

3 Perimeter = ▢ cm
4 Area = ▢ cm²
   (2cm × 2cm square)

5 Perimeter = ▢ cm
6 Area = ▢ cm²
   (4cm × 2cm rectangle)

7 Perimeter = ▢ cm
8 Area = ▢ cm²
   (5cm × 2cm parallelogram)

(Compound shape: B = 1cm × 6cm, A = 6cm × 2cm)

9 Perimeter A = ▢ cm
10 Area A = ▢ cm²
11 Perimeter B = ▢ cm
12 Area B = ▢ cm²
13 Perimeter compound shape = ▢ cm
14 Area compound shape = ▢ cm²

15 The area of the compound shape is Area A + Area B. Why is the perimeter of the compound shape less than Perimeter A + Perimeter B?

_____
_____

Use Edgar's map opposite to write down the correct coordinates. Write the coordinate from the horizontal axis first and then the vertical.

1 City Park   ____,____
2 Smile Street   ____,____
3 Building site   ____,____
4 Police station   ____,____
5 Newspaper office   ____,____
6 TV station   ____,____
7 P's palace   ____,____
8 Helipad   ____,____
9 Jail   ____,____
10 City Hall   ____,____

11 There is a statue of a previous Mayor on the island in the middle of the big roundabout. What are the coordinates?

____,____

12 The goodies hide in a tunnel, which begins 3 squares to the right of the building site. What are the coordinates?

____,____

13 The TV station and newspaper office share a car park, which lies between the 2 buildings. In which square is the car park?

____,____

14 P gets her first TV interview halfway between her palace and the TV station. In which square does it take place?

____,____

15 Before Ezzo heads to the jail to free Christabell and Whiffy, he stops at City Hall. From there, which square does he cross to get to the jail?

____,____

P and Edgar jumped into their car. Flob put his foot on the accelerator. Suddenly, Ezzo leapt onto the bonnet. Flob jammed on the brakes, startled.

Edgar activated his clever bow tie, which shot out like a long arm and grabbed Ezzo with its metal hand, dropping him on the ground.

"Step on it, Flob!" P shouted.

Then Christabell appeared, trailing glue from her gadget. The car spun round on the glue, but Flob reved it up and managed to pull out of the stickiness.

The baddies sped off, but then Flob noticed Waldo sitting right in the middle of the road, looking up at him with big, shiny, loveable eyes.

"Run him down!" Edgar shouted.

"I couldn't!" Flob cried, and swerved. The car veered off the road and ended up in a ditch. Police cars roared in to surround it.

P, Edgar and Flob were marched away. As Flob got into the police car, a pink note fell from his pocket. It read "Please help us. You know we didn't do it. Love Christabell."

Edgar is nasty enough to try and obstruct the course of justice and hurt Ezzo and Waldo. This won't look good when the police get hold of him. Add the bow tie.

 ## Decimal fractions

The baddies should realise the game's up, but being able to see a situation clearly isn't always easy in maths, either. A decimal and a fraction can represent the same number and you need to be able to tell when they match.

$$\frac{1}{4} = 0.25 \qquad \frac{1}{2} = 0.5 \qquad \frac{1}{10} = 0.1$$

Line graphs

Police speed cameras tracking P and Edgar' record its speed as it starts up, skids on the glue and spins into the ditch. Their graph displays the data. Graphs are an easy way to display data as a picture of what the data represents.

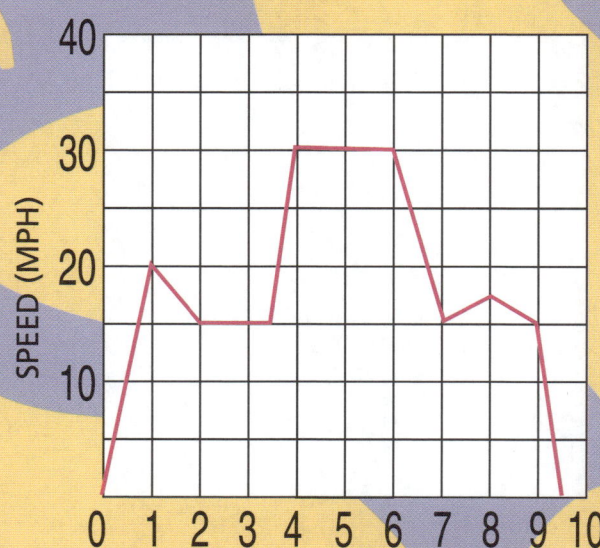

(MPH stands for miles per hour.)

Use lines to join the matching fractions and decimals.

1. $\frac{1}{2}$
2. 5.5
3. 0.2
4. 0.08
5. $\frac{3}{10}$
6. $\frac{71}{100}$
7. $\frac{3}{4}$
8. 3.25

$3\frac{1}{4}$
2.07
$\frac{2}{10}$
0.75
1.4
$2\frac{2}{100}$
$1\frac{3}{4}$
$\frac{8}{100}$
$1\frac{1}{2}$
0.3
0.71
4.30
0.50
$2\frac{3}{4}$
$\frac{1}{100}$

9. $1\frac{2}{5}$
10. 2.75
11. 2.02
12. $4\frac{3}{10}$
13. $2\frac{7}{100}$
14. 0.01
15. 1.75

Use the data on the police's graph to write down answers to these questions.

1. Just after Flob starts the car, Ezzo jumps on the bonnet and Flob jams on the brakes. How many seconds after the car has started does this happen? _____
2. Before Ezzo jumped on the car, how fast was it travelling? _____
3. The car then slowed to 15mph as it was stuck in glue, but for how long? _____
4. During what period of time was this? _____
5. At what point did the car reach its fastest speed? _____
6. How fast was this? _____
7. How long did the car maintain this speed? _____
8. What happened in the story that caused the speed to drop rapidly? _____
9. How low did the speed drop at this point? _____
10. How long did it take to drop to this speed? _____
11. How long after starting did the car reach this speed? _____
12. After this, how long did Flob struggle to control the car? _____
13. Was it travelling at a steady speed during this period? _____
14. How many seconds after it first started did the car swerve into the ditch? _____
15. At what speed was it travelling when it entered the ditch? _____

"The Real Heroes of Monster City!" read the newspaper headlines next day, as pictures of the Smile Street crew looked out from the front pages. When the friendly monsters returned home, they found Smile Street decorated with flags. There were lots of monsters standing in the streets, but this time they were cheering and asking for autographs.

The Mayor of Monster City declared a Smile Street Hero Day and there was a parade through the town, with the friends waving from the top of a bus. Meanwhile P, Edgar and Flob went on trial. P and Edgar were found guilty and imprisoned. Flob was let off with a warning.

"Who gave the police that tip-off about P and Edgar's crimes?" Ezzo asked.

"Someone who didn't want us to go to jail," Christabell replied innocently.

"You mean someone who couldn't bear the idea of YOU going to jail?" Ezzo grinned. "Someone who blushes every time you speak to him? Someone who knows just what P and Edgar get up to? Someone beginning with F, perhaps?"

P and Edgar have got what they deserve. Add the police photo of the baddies as the final piece of evidence and to wrap up the case.

29 Frequency tables

Christabell has been keeping a record of all the times the goodies are mentioned each day in Monster City's newspapers. She is presenting her data as a frequency chart, which shows the number of newspapers giving them 0–5, 6–10, 11–15 and 16–20 mentions.

number of mentions			
0–5	6–10	11–15	16–20

30 Mode and range

P and Edgar will be spending a lot of time with Monster City's worst crooks and villains. The lists to the right give information about the number of years being served by inmates in different wings of the jail.

Finding the range of numbers like these helps you to see the difference between the longest and shortest sentence. The range is the difference between the largest and smallest numbers in a set.

Finding the mode tells you what sentence is most commonly being served. The mode is the most commonly occurring number in a set of numbers.

3 6 3 9 12

Range 12 − 3 = 9
Mode 3

Use the information in Christabell's table to write answers to questions 1 to 11. Then draw the contents for questions 12 to 15.

1 How many newspapers made 6–10 mentions? _____
2 How many newspapers made 16–20 mentions? _____
3 How many newspapers made 0–5 mentions? _____
4 How many newspapers made 11–15 mentions? _____
5 How many mentions were made altogether in all the papers? _____
6 How many newspapers made up to 10 mentions? _____
7 How many made 11–20 mentions? _____
8 How many made 0–15 mentions? _____
9 How many made 6–20 mentions? _____
10 What is the most common range for mentions: 0–5, 6–10, 11–15 or 16–20? _____
11 What is the least common? _____

Today's papers have arrived. 11 have 0–5 mentions, 16 have 6–10 mentions, 27 have 11–15 mentions and 9 have 16–20 mentions.

12 Draw the contents of the 0–5 column.
13 Draw the contents of the 6–10 column.
14 Draw the contents of the 11–15 column.
15 Draw the contents of the 16–20 column.

Write down the range and mode of these numbers showing information on sentences being served by inmates in different wings of the jail.

| 7 3 5 7 9 7 |

1 What is the range? _6_
2 What is the mode? _7_

| 9 40 35 41 35 35 |

9 What is the range? _____
10 What is the mode? _____

| 30 6 2 30 30 32 |

3 What is the range? _30_
4 What is the mode? _30_

| 50 25 50 12 25 50 |

11 What is the range? _____
12 What is the mode? _____

| 12 9 12 15 15 12 |

5 What is the range? _____
6 What is the mode? _____

| 13 12 11 13 7 9 |

13 What is the range? _____
14 What is the mode? _____
15 One of the prisoners on this wing has his sentences reduced from 13 to 12 years. Now what is the mode? _____

| 6 3 5 2 6 1 |

7 What is the range? _____
8 What is the mode? _____

Answers

Test 1 Sequences
1. 0.2 0.4 0.6 0.8 1 1.2 1.4
2. 0.1 0.2 0.3 0.4 0.5 0.6 0.7
3. 0.5 1 1.5 2 2.5 3 3.5
4. 1.75 1.5 1.25 1 0.75 0.5 0.25
5. 1 4 8 13 19 26 34
6. 0 3 6 9 12 15 18
7. 0 2 4 6 8 10 12
8. 4 8 12 16 20 24 28
9. 7 14 21 28 35 42 49
10. 3 7 11 15 19 23 27
11. 5 10 15 20 25 30 35
12. 2.2 2.0 1.8 1.6 1.4 1.2 1
13. 12.5 12 11.5 11 10.5 10 9.5
14. 11.4 11.3 11.2 11.1 11 10.9 10.8
15. 3.75 3.5 3.25 3.0 2.75 2.5 2.25

Test 2 Multiplying and dividing decimals
1. 3
2. 0.2
3. 1.25
4. 0.06
5. 0.33
6. 1.989
7. 1.401
8. 7
9. 3.4
10. 94.2
11. 0.2
12. 9.21
13. 10.48
14. 24.23
15. 99.91

Test 3 Equivalent fractions
The matching pairs are:
1. $1\frac{5}{6} = \frac{11}{6}$
2. $11\frac{1}{2} = \frac{23}{2}$
3. $2\frac{3}{4} = \frac{11}{4}$
4. $1\frac{18}{23} = \frac{41}{23}$
5. $2\frac{14}{15} = \frac{44}{15}$
6. $4\frac{1}{8} = \frac{33}{8}$
7. $8\frac{1}{2} = \frac{17}{2}$
8. $12\frac{2}{3} = \frac{38}{3}$
9. $4\frac{2}{7} = \frac{30}{7}$
10. $9\frac{2}{7} = \frac{65}{7}$
11. $6\frac{2}{5} = \frac{32}{5}$
12. $1\frac{17}{35} = \frac{52}{35}$
13. $9\frac{1}{4} = \frac{37}{4}$
14. $11\frac{1}{7} = \frac{78}{7}$
15. $14\frac{2}{3} = \frac{44}{3}$

Test 4 Positive and negative numbers
1. 7
2. 24
3. 93
4. 227
5. 463
6. 228
7. 334
8. 9
9. 93
10. 42
11. 70
12. 62
13. 14
14. 72
15. 91

Test 5 Probability
1. 2 in 8 or 1 in 4
2. 6 in 8 or 3 in 4
3. 3 in 6 or 1 in 2
4. 2 in 6 or 1 in 3
5. 1 in 7
6. 2 in 7
7. 3 in 9 or 1 in 3
8. 3 in 8
9. 1 in 10
10. 2 in 10 or 1 in 5
11. 1 in 3
12. 1 in 2
13. 1 in 52
14. 4 in 52 or 1 in 13
15. 13 in 52 or 1 in 4

Test 6 Ratio and proportion
1. 2:5
2. 2 in 7
3. 2:3
4. 2 in 5
5. 2:2
6. 2 in 4
7. 2:4
8. 4 in 6 or 2 in 3
9. 3:5
10. 5 in 8
11. 2:6
12. 6 in 8 or 3 in 4
13. 3:5
14. 3 in 8
15. 5 in 8

Test 7 Time zones
1. 06:15
2. 08:30
3. 13:45
4. 18:30
5. 23:12
6. 01:11
7. 16:42
8. 23:01
9. 20:36
10. 17:10
11. 15:32
12. 19:53
13. 16:47
14. 21:21
15. 02:37

Test 8 Percentages
1. 25
2. 100
3. 45
4. 60
5. 190
6. £60
7. £20
8. £3.25
9. £66
10. 94
11. 1.5m or 150cm
12. 0.25m or 25cm
13. 1.2kg or 1200g
14. 0.03m or 3cm
15. 0.12m or 12cm

Test 9 Angles
1. 45°
2. 90°
3. 180°
4. 90°
5. 270°
6. 315°
7. 45°
8. 180°
9. 315°
10. 90°
11. 180°
12. 360°
13. 225°
14. 270°
15. 45°

Test 10 Ordering mixed numbers
1. 2.321 3.021 3.102 3.201
2. 12.123 12.312 13.132 13.321
3. 8.119 8.189 8.911 8.919
4. 7.114 7.143 7.314 7.341
5. 21.012 21.021 21.210 22.110
6. 90.188 90.881 91.180 91.881
7. 11.013 13.013 13.130 13.301
8. 0.031 0.130 0.301 0.310
9. 2.001 2.002 2.012 2.021
10. 0.001 0.010 0.011 1.001
11. 0.303 3.030 3.033 3.330
12. 17.007 17.070 17.077 17.770
13. 15.009 15.090 15.900 19.050
14. 4.050 4.055 4.500 4.505
15. 91.009 91.909 91.910 99.091

Test 11 Word problems
1. 18
2. 16
3. 4
4. 4.5
5. 25m
6. 3.5 seconds
7. Ezzo
8. 40 seconds
9. 84kg
10. 20g or 0.02kg
11. 400g or 0.4kg
12. 15 seconds
13. 10 seconds
14. no
15. 2m per second

Test 12 Reflecting shapes

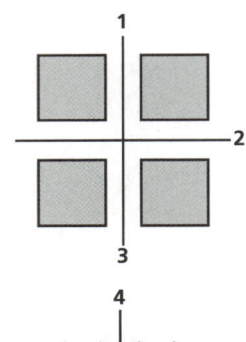
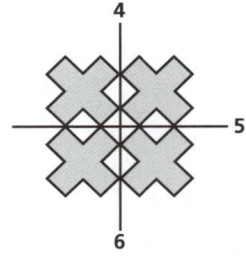
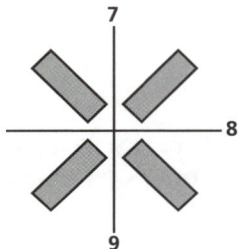
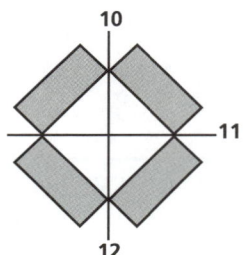
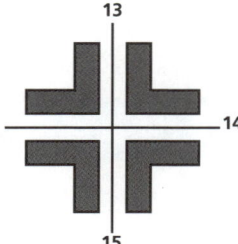

Test 13 Brackets
1. 10
2. 14
3. 72
4. 5
5. 22
6. 2
7. 13
8. 32
9. 72
10. 7
11. 3
12. 7
13. 3
14. 3
15. 12